Contents

An Escort to Heaven

The doctor's words ricocheted through my mind: "Unfortunately, Jake didn't make it." I slammed the phone down in disbelief. Sobbing, I collapsed on the counter.

My fiancé grabbed my purse and rushed me to his truck. By the time we got to the hospital, the sight of my five-year-old son Garrett was a shock. The blood from the wounds on his face had already turned a crusty black. At first glance, it looked like all of his teeth had been knocked out from the impact.

"Hi Garrett," I said as I forced a smile and leaned down to kiss his forehead. "Where did you get this stuffed bear? He sure is cute."

"From the ambulance man," Garrett managed to say through his swollen jaw.

Like most young boys, Garrett was fascinated by emergency responders. His favorite TV program was *Rescue 911*. Before the show started, he would line up all of his electronic emergency vehicles on the carpet in front of the TV. His collection of fire trucks, police cars and ambulances were ready for action. I never imagined he would be a victim in his own episode.

Suddenly the curtains opened and the doctor entered the room. "We need to check for internal injuries. Since Garrett can't swallow the contrast dye, we'll need to insert a tube up his nose and down his throat to inject the dye for the X-ray. Would you like to stay in the room and hold his hand?"

"Of course." I gulped, fighting back tears. Never mind that I couldn't even watch my own blood being drawn.

The rest of the day was a blur. Between all the phone calls and the multitude of visitors I barely remember a thing except that an odd but welcome sense of peace began to settle on me. Later that day, the doctor gave us the first bit of good news.

"Garrett has a hairline fracture to his jaw but the X-rays show no internal injuries."

The swelling in Garrett's face prevented much of an expression, but I could tell he was trying to smile. He didn't want me to worry. Soon, he drifted off to sleep.

The next morning, I dropped little squirts of juice into Garrett's mouth with a baby eye-dropper. "What's wrong, Mommy?"

"Nothing," I lied. Despite the peace I felt, the truth was I didn't have a clue how I was going to tell him about his two-year-old brother Jake.

"Why don't you wait until Garrett asks about Jake?" my friends advised. Initially, that sounded like a good plan, but four days later he still hadn't asked.

With the funeral approaching, my fiancé was concerned. "Do you want me to talk to him?" John asked.

"No." I sighed. "I have to do this myself."

Garrett's face brightened as I entered his room. "Look Mommy! Bruce brought me some more stuffed animals. And the Transformer I wanted — Optimus Prime."

"That's nice, honey." I hesitantly pulled up a chair to his bedside.

"Garrett," I began.

"Yeah, Mommy?"

My body felt suddenly paralyzed. "What would you say if I told you…," I stalled, gasping for air. "It's Jake. Jake didn't make it." Tears streamed down my face. I couldn't even look up.

"Mom, I already know."

"You already know?" My jaw dropped. "What do you mean, you already know?"

"After the accident, I got to go to heaven with Jake." Garrett swooped Optimus Prime into the air. He made gun sounds as he beat up his invisible enemies. "Jake got to go in but God told me it wasn't my time."

Suddenly I was on the edge of my seat. "What was heaven like?"

"Mommy!" Garrett's eyes squinted with apparent irritation. He set his Transformer down. A bewildered look spread across his face. "Mommy! I can't tell you that!"

"Why not?" I insisted.

"It's a surprise!"

"I'm sure God won't mind if you tell me, Garrett. He'll understand — I'm your mother."

"No, Mommy, I can't!"

"Why not?"

"Cuz. God told me it's a secret."

He went back to playing with his toys while I sat back in my chair flabbergasted. Garrett sure picked a good time to start keeping secrets. In the past he flunked confidentiality, but now his lips were locked.

The peace that Garrett felt magnified my own. We both spoke at Jake's funeral. I held the microphone while he shared his story about escorting his little brother to heaven in front of hundreds of attendees. In the days and weeks following his release from the hospital, I tried to squeeze details out of Garrett, but he never uttered another clue. His childlike trust amazed me, yet I fought skepticism. Did Garrett really take a trip to heaven or was his story a figment of his five-year-old imagination?

Preschoolers can make up some enchanting stories. If it was make-believe, however, it worked for him. He didn't grieve like the grief recovery books predicted. He never had a nightmare about the accident. And even though his biological father received a deferred sentence for negligent homicide for driving under the influence of several narcotics, Garrett held no bitterness toward his dad. Even so, I pried and pried to get him to open up about his trip to heaven.

Until I found the reason for his peculiar silence.

One day, I was reading my morning devotional and came across a story in the Bible about a man who had been to heaven. He couldn't describe what he saw because it was a secret. I was spellbound. In the book of Second Corinthians, the apostle Paul says that he was caught up in the "third heaven" where he heard inexpressible things — things that man was not permitted to tell.

Paul experienced the same kind of secret quest that Garrett had witnessed.

I lingered over the verses for a moment. What Garrett saw, he wasn't permitted to tell. It really was a secret. It wasn't a fairy tale — it was a faith tale.

I closed my Bible. My doubts had finally vanished. Who was I to contend with a divine mystery? Awestruck, I realized that his journey to heaven empowered him with peace in the midst of disaster. Never again will I doubt the faith of a child, nor God's ability to provide peace in the midst of tragedy.

Especially to his precious little children.

• • •

Jake's death changed my destiny. I started writing because of the peace and joy I experienced in the midst of sorrow. In a way, Jake's legacy lives on in me. As for Garrett — he is nineteen and although he still speaks little of his trip to heaven, his countenance of peace has never left. I know God has a strong purpose for the secret he entrusted with Garrett that day. As much as I long to understand more, one thing I know for sure — heaven is flowing with peace and joy, because Garrett came back with a lifetime supply.

~Christy Johnson

The Telephone

"Sue, listen to me." I pleaded with my twin sister. With tears in my eyes I took another sip of my strong hot coffee and tried to convince my sister once again to contact my neighbor, Nellie.

I leaned forward in my chair facing the floral sofa where Sue often sat when she stopped by for morning coffee. "Remember when I told you about my neighbor, Nellie? Please," I begged. "Go see her!"

Morning conversations with my sister were nothing new. We had been doing this for years. We lived in the same town. So getting together for coffee in the morning was easy.

Many times after taking my children to the bus stop in the morning, I returned to my house and would hear Sue's cheerful voice leaving a message on my answering machine. "Hey Donna, just put the kids on the bus. Thought I'd stop by for a cup of coffee. Give me a call."

We cherished our morning chats. We talked about our families, faith and current events. We shared recipes, home decorating ideas and any concerns we might have. We gave each other advice and comfort.

One morning I shared with Sue an amazing story about Nellie. My friend Denise had shared the story with me. Sue was fascinated. But now she didn't seem to remember Nellie or the story at all.

Sadness filled my voice. I took a deep breath and reminded Sue again, "Denise told me when her mom passed away after a long illness that Nellie, our neighbor, whom I had never met, called Denise on the phone late one night. Nellie said, 'Denise, your mom just came to see me. She wants me to tell you, thank you for taking such good care of her.' Denise told me Nellie was a medium."

"Sue, are you listening to me?" But of course I only heard silence. How could I know if Sue heard me or not when she had passed away two months ago?

I thought back to the morning when Sue phoned me early, canceling our coffee date. "Hey Donna, I'm not feeling well today. I have a bit of a headache. Let's catch up later."

But we never did. Within the hour Sue had a massive stroke and passed away a few days later.

Now I sat alone in the family room and drank the last drops of my coffee. I felt foolish sitting there and talking to an empty sofa and yet I had so much to say.

"Suzy, I miss you so much," I said aloud. "I have so much to tell you. We finished the bathroom upstairs. Remember I was decorating it in a Bermuda beach theme? It's pink, bright and beautiful! I wish you could see it. You would love it."

I continued. "I bought Stephanie a heart locket for her birthday. I had it engraved with

'I Hope You Dance,' your favorite song." Sue had three young children. Stephanie was the oldest who had just turned sixteen. I chose a gift that I imagined Sue would have selected for her if she could.

"I wish I knew if you could hear me!" I began to sob. "Are you there? Are you okay?"

I did not mention to anyone, including Denise, that I was begging my deceased sister to go to Nellie. I really wanted to appear strong for my family and friends. Yet privately I continued to send up this prayer of desperation. My faith had always been strong, but now I needed some confirmation. I needed to hear from my sister!

Exhausted, I got up. I wiped my tears, picked up my coffee mug and placed it in the kitchen sink. I walked through the house and gently picked up my sister's red and black sweater that I kept on my chair. I gave it a hug. It gave me comfort. I could still smell her Vanilla Fields perfume. "I wish you were here, Sue," I whispered.

Later in the week, I was resting on my bed. It had been another rough day of dealing with my grief. "Please God," I prayed. "Help Sue connect with Nellie."

Suddenly the phone rang. "Hi Donna, this is Nellie. You don't know me but I'm a friend of your friend Denise." My heart leaped!

"Oh yes, I know all about you!" I said. My heart was pounding.

"Do you know about my gift?" Nellie asked cautiously.

"I do. Denise told me how her mother came to you. I totally believe in your gift!"

"Well that's good because your sister is driving me crazy." She laughed. "For the past few weeks she has been asking me to call you. I wanted to check with Denise first to see if it was okay. I was planning to call you later today but your sister was pleading with me, 'Will you please call my sister now!'"

Nellie jumped right into sharing Sue's messages. "Sue is showing me a bright pink room. She says to tell you she sees it and it's beautiful."

Ah, the new bathroom. I smiled.

"Your sister is also showing me a locket and says, 'Thank you.'"

My heart filled with joy thinking of Stephanie's birthday locket.

"One more thing," Nellie added. "Your sister is showing me a red and black sweater. She says it is meant to give you comfort."

This message really got to me. Sue was with me when I was holding her sweater.

Finally Nellie said, "Donna, your sister wants you to know she loves you, she's proud of you and is always with you."

I did not hear from Nellie again until the late fall. She phoned me one afternoon with another message from Sue, one I did not understand. "Sue says go ahead and honor her."

I told Nellie I had no idea what it meant. "Honor her? Sue was always so humble." Nellie assured me, "Donna, tuck this message away for later. See what happens."

In early December Sue's husband Bill and I were talking. "The funeral home called. They are having a memorial service for those who have lost loved ones this past year. The kids can make an ornament to honor their mom and place it on their Christmas tree."

Bill was concerned. "Do you think the kids will be okay going back to the funeral home for this memorial?" I remembered Sue's words, "Go ahead and honor me."

I turned to Bill and smiled. "Let them. It will be okay."

The children went to the service and honored their mom. It was one of many steps in their healing process.

I called Nellie to thank her for using her amazing gift to help others. Nellie responded with a humble little laugh. "Donna, I am just a telephone that connects family and friends with their loved ones in Heaven."

Yes, I thought, a telephone ... with a great connection.

~Donna Teti

One Last Visit Before the Light

I was driving home from work and I felt troubled. I was thinking that we should have gone to Phoenix on Memorial Day, but I had just started a new job so we hadn't gone. My mother-in-law had been diagnosed with breast cancer shortly after our wedding and given six months to live. But with good doctors and care in Phoenix, she was still alive three years later. Natalie, at sixty-three, was a tiny four-foot-something, gentle, loving woman. Her favorite poem to quote ended with, "Love in your heart wasn't put there to stay. Love isn't love 'till you give it away." She loved her three grand-children with every fiber of her being. She was thrilled when I had Nicholas; she just couldn't get enough of him.

My in-laws made a habit of summering in

San Diego to escape the Arizona heat and to be near us, except this summer. Natalie instead asked us to bring Nicky to Phoenix over Memorial Day weekend. She didn't tell us how sick she was, not wanting us to worry. But if we had known, we would have gone.

It was 4:45 p.m. I had stopped briefly at home and was about to go to the sitter's house to get Nicky when the phone rang. It was my sister-in-law.

"Lisa, I'm glad I caught you," Helaine said in a voice choked with grief. "Mom just passed away at 4:30. Marcia and I were with her at the hospital. Can you guys come?"

"Sure," I reassured her. "I'll call the airline and get the baby. We'll be there as soon as we can."

Minutes later, I arrived at the babysitter's house. Dee-dee, a Navy wife, ran a home day care to keep busy while her husband was away at sea. It was a perfect place for Nicky. Dee-dee was sensitive and caring, treating her day care kids as her own. But today, Dee-dee was pale and visibly shaken when she answered the door.

"What's wrong, Dee?" I asked as I stepped inside. I felt an immediate tingling of panic for my son.

"It's Nicky. He did something strange a few minutes ago," Dee-dee replied nervously. "He was sitting out back in the sandbox, playing with his favorite truck. All of a sudden, he dropped it and looked up — at nothing, just up at the air, the sky, for a minute. And he said, 'Bye-bye, Grandma. Bye-bye, Grandma. Bye-bye,' three times, just like that.

"Then, I got the eeriest feeling," she said, rubbing her upper arms with her hands. "I felt like I was being watched by something. I ran out there and picked him up and brought him inside."

I felt a flush of heat rush over my body and face.

Dee-dee continued, "I knew you were probably on your way because I looked at the clock there in the kitchen and it was 4:30. But why he was saying 'Grandma', I don't know."

"Oh, Lord," I said, rushing over and grabbing Nicky off the floor. "My mother-in-law just passed away in Phoenix. I just got the call before I drove here."

Dee-dee put her hand on the wall to steady herself. She was a devout Baptist and regular churchgoer. "Praise Jesus, Amen!" Dee-dee shouted. "Praise the Lord, Jesus! It was her spirit!"

It was obvious early on that my son was gifted. I know most parents think their kids are gifted, but Nicky always hit his milestones before he normally should. By eighteen months old, he was fully conversational. You could ask him questions and get complete, coherent answers.

I sat the tiny boy on the sofa in the living room. Kneeling beside him, I asked Nicky why he said goodbye to his grandmother. He matter-of-factly explained that she had come to see him because she was going away. He said that she told him she loved him very much and wanted to see him.

I asked him where Grandma was. He pointed, indicating the backyard. "She was outside, over there, floating in the air."

Then I asked if Grandma did anything. Nick said, "Grandma talked, but not out loud. She talked in that little voice inside my head. She said, 'I love you,' and she wanted to kiss me, but she couldn't."

"Why?" I asked.

"Because, she had blood on her mouth," he said. "And then she went up to the clouds."

Dee-dee blanched. I tried to keep a calm exterior, not showing the alarm I felt. I didn't want Nick to cry; I wanted answers.

"And what did Grandma look like?" I queried further.

Nick explained in his "big man" voice, "She was wearing a dress with little flowers all over it and she had wires on her arms."

Dee-dee and I were dumbfounded. Natalie so much wanted to see him before she passed over that she came to him before going to the

Light. I believe that distance and time are immaterial for the spirit once it leaves the body. She wanted to see her grandson and let him know of her love.

My husband and I got to Phoenix later that night. We were at my father-in-law's home with my husband's sisters. I recounted the story about Nicky and Natalie. A stunned silence fell over the family. Helaine said that at the time of death, her mom was wearing a hospital gown with tiny blue flowers on it and she had intravenous tubes in her arms. A therapist took her respirator out, tearing her lip slightly in the process. "She had a little trickle of blood on the corner of her mouth," Helaine said, stunned. "But how…"

My father-in-law realized how Nick knew. Nine years earlier, Bob had a massive cardiac arrest and near-death experience. He spent years reading about and researching these experiences, and taught us all about the spirit's ability to travel and the Light of God that one crosses into at the time of death. Bob made us firmly believe, "Death is the gate of life. It's not an end. The soul goes on." And Natalie showed us that.

~Lisa Wojcik

The Unforgotten

I've never been much of a believer in the supernatural, but my late husband, Ken Wilson, definitely was. Though he disdained stories about zombies and mummies, or werewolves and vampires, tales of psychic phenomena thoroughly mesmerized him.

For years he'd collected books on astral projection, parapsychology, telepathy, hauntings and possessions. He subscribed to *Fate Magazine*, and read it from cover to cover. And aside from Westerns, his favorite movie was *Ghost*, with *The Sixth Sense* running a close second. Ken didn't espouse any particular religion, but I've always felt that if there had been a Spiritualist church nearby, he would have been a regular.

A few years ago, Ken was diagnosed with

pancreatic cancer and he took the news with astonishingly good humor.

"I'm ready to visit the other side," he said, and then proceeded to regale me with yarns about how he'd come back to haunt me and both of his beloved dogs.

"There's no good reason not to believe in an afterlife," he explained. "Harry Houdini did, Arthur Conan Doyle did, and I do, too. I'll find a way. I may not communicate directly, but I'm certain I'll be able to let you know I'm still around and thinking of you."

"Just don't do anything too spooky," I pleaded. "I don't want howls and squeaks coming off the walls of the bedroom. You know what a scaredy cat I am. I didn't sleep for a week after we watched *The Blair Witch Project*."

"I wouldn't want to frighten you, baby, but I do want you to remember me and that I'm not completely gone. My body might not be there, but my spirit will be."

The morning he died, I thought about what he'd promised. I'd heard that recent widows often feel the presence of their departed spouses in the corridors. But all morning our house felt completely empty as I wandered its rooms and hallways, wondering if I'd ever find the time and energy to clear Ken's clothes from the closets.

Then that afternoon, the dogs escaped. The young man who had come to mow our lawn absentmindedly had left a gate open. Ordinarily when the pair broke loose they'd be gone for hours, but this time the dogs dragged themselves home in less than thirty minutes. And though they usually head for the river and a swim, this time their fur remained completely dry. Nonetheless, they both plopped down on the tiled entryway, acting as exhausted as if they'd swum the English Channel. They stared at me with the most sheepish expression that a pair of canine faces can assume. I suddenly believed Ken had tracked them down, scolded them and sent them home. Moreover, the house no longer felt so empty. Ken's spirit had returned.

Not long after, a writer and editor acquaintance launched a new career as a psychic. He knew I'd been recently widowed, and offered me a telephone consultation. He told me that Ken's spirit indeed was present on my property, and that it frequently walked around the backyard with the dogs. I believe that's why Natty, who was particularly attached to Ken, lies out there for hours looking blissfully zoned out. He especially demands to go out at twilight and comes in only reluctantly when I'm ready for bed.

Ken had reminded me of Houdini's avowal to contact people from beyond. I don't think I've ever heard that the magician managed to succeed. But twice in the couple of years since Ken's death, I've found books overturned from the case that's adjacent to my writing desk in the family room.

The first incident, about a month after Ken's death, involved *Over Tumbled Graves* by Jess Walter. Ken and I met this Northeast Washington writer when he came to our local

Colville library to give a talk. Ken had accompanied me when my book group dined with Walter before his presentation. This was a book Ken had read and an author he had met. I shivered as I set the book back in place.

Then about a year later I spied a second book on the floor, apparently knocked loose from the same bookcase. This time it was Faye Kellerman's *The Forgotten*. Both of us had been fans of this novelist, and had frequently discussed her mysteries. I couldn't help but reflect on the title of this particular book as I tucked it back into place. Some time had elapsed since my husband's death. Could he be sending me a message from beyond that he worried I'd begun to forget him?

I'm not certain I'm ready yet to declare myself a believer in psychic phenomena, but this is the kind of spooky coincidence that Ken adored. I've always doubted there's any literal heaven populated by angels and filled with harps and fluffy clouds. But Ken was convinced that some aspect of the human personality or mind survives death and continues to exist on a spirit plane. As for me, I've always believed in the power of prayer. So that night I said a special prayer for my very special late husband.

I asked that he be guaranteed that he's not forgotten. Not now. Not ever. I prayed he'd be reassured that his portrait still hangs in our bedroom, and informed that I've also put up the framed maps of ancient Briton that he never got around to displaying.

I added that I'd weed around his Asian lilies the next afternoon and sprinkle them with deer repellent. I vowed that on his birthday I'd haul down his special ceramic cup and pour him a brandy Manhattan and place it by the lilies. I wanted him to know that I'd think of something special to commemorate him on what would have been our tenth anniversary.

Finally, I conveyed that I'd continue to write about him and our life together. Ken Wilson wouldn't be forgotten at all. He'd live on in my stories, just as his spirit continues to inhabit our home. He'd be eternally "The Unforgotten."

Every morning I still cast a hopeful glance at the floor in front of the bookcase. I would be neither surprised nor frightened if I received yet another message from heaven, wherever and whatever it may be.

~Terri Elders

The Message

I woke up with an uneasy feeling. Something was niggling at me — a thought swirling in my mind that I couldn't quite grasp. I looked at the clock on my night table, remembering that I was due at the office for an early meeting. I jumped up and went into the shower. My throat began to constrict and my stomach cramped and churned. A sure sign of an impending anxiety attack. Why? What was bothering me? I didn't know, but I was definitely experiencing discomfort.

Snatches of a dream surfaced as I headed towards the subway station. Parts of the dream came to me as I sat on the train. In the dream I was walking on a street in Brooklyn and I saw two of my mom's dearest friends heading towards me. We greeted one another, and her friend Tillie said, "We're looking for your mom, but she isn't home."

"Oh, she's probably at the grocery store. Why not wait in the lobby? I'm sure she'll be home any minute. It's getting dark."

"Okay," Tillie and Ann answered in unison.

As I left them, I thought how strange it was to see them. I couldn't recall for the moment whether they were still living or had passed away.

I woke up.

Instinctively, I knew this dream was symbolic. A sense of foreboding engulfed me. I felt chilled and my hands were cold. I was having trouble breathing. My windpipe was closing. I concentrated on calming myself, visualizing my throat relaxing and attempting to take deep cleansing breaths, as in yoga.

My brain kept telling me this was important. That it was one of those dreams I needed to pay attention to and understand. I felt anxious and pressured, my body's way of signaling this was significant.

I exited the train and slowly climbed the stairs to the street, conscious of my ragged breathing. At the top of the staircase, I was seriously gasping for air. My shoulders felt heavy, as if I was carrying a heavy backpack.

I hailed a taxi to go the three blocks to my office. Think! Think! Think! What was the message? It was urgent I understood the meaning.

No sooner had I sat down at my desk, my assistant said, "Wendy's on the phone." Wendy was my mom's aide and companion. She was with my mom from early morning to after dinner.

"Wendy, hello …"

"Mrs. L., something's terribly wrong with your mom. She's sitting up in bed, wild-eyed and scrunched up by the headboard, but she can't see me or hear me. She's talking, like foreign. I can't understand anything she's saying. I don't know what to do. It's scary seeing her like this. What should I do?"

Oh my God. I was an idiot. How much more crystal clear could the message have been? Tillie and Ann were letting me know they'd come to escort Mom to the other side.

"Wendy, I want you to hang up and call 911, immediately. I think she's having a stroke. She's speaking Hungarian. Make sure you have them take her to Lutheran Medical Center. If they give you any problems, call my sister and let her speak to them. I'll call Dorothy and let her know what's going on. I'll meet you at the hospital. Call them now!"

I dialed my sister, Dorothy, who was a nurse at Lutheran, and only fifteen minutes away from Mom's apartment. After I hung up with her, I called my husband Alan. His office was on the same floor as mine. I told Francine, my assistant, to cancel everything on my schedule.

By the time we reached the hospital, Dorothy was standing by the bed as Mom lay there with her eyes closed. She remained unresponsive to our voices or touch.

"The doctor believes she's had a massive stroke. If she survives, she'll be in a vegetative state," Dorothy whispered to us.

I continued to hold her hand, stroking her forehead as I talked quietly to her, trying to will her to respond.

We had her moved to a private room and we took turns being with her for the first week. When we weren't with her, Wendy and her mom stayed with her. We wanted someone who loved her to be there as much as possible.

Both Dorothy and I agreed that it would be far better for her to leave us than survive in a vegetative state. Mom was fiercely independent and never would have wanted to live in a suspended state.

On Friday, the end of the second week, I woke up crying. I called my sister and told her we were going straight to the hospital. "If you have anything to say to Mom, do it now. She's leaving us at sunset tonight."

"Did you have another dream? Or are you feeling something?" Dorothy asked.

Over the years my sister had become accustomed to hearing about my dreams and premonitions.

"Both Dad and Aunt Belle died on a Friday night at the start of the Sabbath. Mom's going to join them tonight. Call your girls and tell them to be there by the afternoon. I didn't have another dream. It was more an awareness and sensing. I was crying when I woke up."

"Okay, I'm not going to argue with you, you're always right when you get like this. See you later."

As the sun began to set, we gathered around her bed, each saying our final farewells. We told her she could let go. "Everybody's there waiting, Dad, Belle, your mom and poppa, your brothers and friends. Tillie and Ann are waiting to greet you and guide you across."

I bent down, whispering in her ear, "Mom, we love you and if you are ready to go, we are ready. It's okay. Go with our blessings and love." I kissed her cheek as I squeezed her hand.

We formed a circle around her. We held hands with each other. We held her hands.

Wendy led us in reciting the twenty-third Psalm.

We watched her, heard her breathing grow slower and shallower. We hardly moved. Calmness permeated.

As the sun set and the Sabbath began, she quietly and peacefully left us.

~Margo Berk-Levine

Heart Attack

"Get up, Jeanne. Get dressed!"

I try to open my eyes, but my lids are stuck closed, as if glued.

"What is it, Pop? What's wrong?"

"Hurry, get dressed. We have to leave now." I rise from the daybed, quickly pull my pants over my pajamas and throw a sweatshirt over my eighteen-year-old frame. My eyes try to adjust to the darkness as I maneuver down the thin hallway in my grandparent's one-bedroom apartment in Flushing, Queens.

"Don't turn on the light," my grandfather says. "Take Grandma's hand and follow me."

"Ed, where are we going? What's wrong?" Grandma asks.

"Just follow me. Don't say a word," he whispers.

I run my hand along the bumpy stucco walls as we pass by the kitchen, into the living room and out the front door. I'm not sure of the time. We quickly leave the apartment and descend the short staircase to the street and then turn right. We pass the well-manicured shrubs that Pop has tended to as property manager since he and Grandma moved there nearly thirty years ago. Walking a little further, we make another right up the narrow path that leads us toward the basement door. I can smell the fresh mint that comes up every year for my grandmother's tea. Clutching the cool, damp, wrought-iron railing, we descend the narrow staircase.

Pop gently grabs Grandma's elbow, guiding her to the basement door. He picks one key from a ring of many, and inserts it. As he opens the outside door to the basement, a hard, stale smell smacks me in the face, waking me to the reality that something is desperately wrong.

As a child, I often played in this basement. Grandma would hang her fresh laundry on what seemed like rows and rows of laundry line. I would go downstairs and play hide-and-seek with her, running in-between Pop's shirts and Grandma's nightgowns, interspersed doilies occasionally falling to the ground.

Pop's workshop is adjacent to the laundry room. It is where he stores his tools and an occasional bottle of schnapps. When I dared to venture off course from the laundry path, I would go to Pop's room. Occasionally I would find the door slightly ajar and I would squeeze my way into his world. Pop spent a lot of time down there, fixing things that needed to be fixed and, I suspect, fixing things that did not need to be fixed. It was his private space where he found refuge.

Once inside the basement, the three of us travel in and out of Grandma's hanging laundry. Each touch of clothing brings a clean, light smell and then we are back to the heavy, stale darkness. We approach Pop's workroom, which is locked. He takes out his ring of keys, and once again, immediately picks the right one.

The door creaks as he slowly opens it. He turns on a small flashlight, the tiny light illuminating our way. I look at Pop and see a look of terror on his face. I have never known my grandfather to be afraid. Indifferent, mad, loving, intoxicated, proud, but never afraid.

He guides us in and starts up a dark stairway. A crackling sound follows behind us. I look at Grandma. She cannot keep up the pace.

Pop looks up and spots a narrow space hidden under the staircase. "Help Grandma in there," he says to me.

Somehow, I am able to pick her up and slide her into the small space. "Grams, stay here and don't make a sound. You must be quiet." She looks so tiny, so frightened. I hate to leave her, but I trust this to be the best course.

"We'll be back for you. You'll be safe here," I promise.

Pop stretches up to touch her hand. "Stay here, Anna. Jeanne will be back for you soon. She will take care of you." We leave my grand-

mother there, hidden from something or someone that I don't know.

Pop and I continue on. Out of nowhere, a
huge shadow appears behind us. Pop pushes
me aside and tells me to run. "Run, Jeanne.
Don't look back. Take care of Grandma. Run."
Despite his warning, I can't help but look
behind me, only to see a massive silhouette lift
my grandfather and then stab him through the
heart.

I spring up in bed, shaking uncontrollable,
crying, and realize I have woken from a nightmare.

I go back to sleep, managing to get in an
hour or so before going to work and then an
afternoon lecture at the local college I am
attending as a freshman. By the time I get to
class, last night's dream has left my immediate
thoughts and my mind is focused on Psychol-
ogy 101. I find my seat among 200-plus stu-
dents and settle in to hear about abnormal
behavior. Midway through the lecture, I stand
up abruptly. My friend sitting next to me grabs

my arm and asks what's wrong. She tugs at me to sit down.

"My grandfather just died," I say almost matter-of-factly and storm out, leaving abnormal behavior behind.

Tears flow as I drive home. I park the car, knowing in my heart that Pop is gone.

Later that night I learn that Pop had died from a heart attack at the same moment I stood up during class. That day, he had worked outside raking leaves and was feeling tired, Grandma said. He had given her a big kiss and laid down on the daybed, arms crossed, with a content look on his face as if he knew. Pop was ready.

After his death, I visited my grandmother as often as I could. She was exhibiting signs of dementia, although back then, it was simply labeled old age. I would visit weekly and we would do her shopping, watch her soaps and play *Scrabble*. I worried about her living alone, so I called daily.

That spring, Grandma had a slight heart

attack. I went to visit her in the hospital. It was a dreary place. She was in a large dim room with rows of patients separated mostly by visitors sitting in short, narrow aisles. I saw her lying in her bed at the far end. Trying to maintain a brave front, I called to her, "Grandma, I'm here." As I approached her bed, I could see she looked anxious.

"What's the matter?" I asked, as she pulled me down next to her on the hospital bed.

"Thank goodness you're okay," she said desperately.

"Grandma, what's the matter? What are you taking about?"

"I thought you were dead. I thought he got you," she whispered loudly.

Figuring that she was hallucinating because of the heart attack, I asked again, "Who got me?"

"That man."

"What man?"

"The man that killed Pop in the basement."

I froze.

"You saved me, Jeanne. You hid me under the staircase. I was so afraid but Pop said you would come back and you did. He said you would come back and take care of me and you have."

I had thought that my dream wasn't real. I had never told my grandmother about it, knowing it would just confuse and upset her, as it had me. It wasn't until I heard her recite the same events, months after my grandfather's death, that I realized that just maybe it had been more than a dream. Just maybe it was Pop's final message asking me to watch over my grandmother and keep her safe.

~Jeanne Blandford

Two More Years

It was March 23, 1992, 4:31 a.m. The shrill ringing of the phone jarred me awake but I hesitated. My husband, Art, stirred beside me, prodding me to answer. My father had been hospitalized for over a month during which time I had returned to my childhood home to step into my father's shoes and take care of my bedridden, partially paralyzed mother. As we feared, it was a nurse at the hospital calling to inform us that my father, Joe Bellinghausen, had died of a heart attack at the age of eighty-seven.

An only child, I had no siblings to consult about taking my mother, Dolly, from her familiar surroundings of eighty-eight years and moving her to Texas. I pondered the wisdom of such a decision, worrying that if she died on my watch soon after, I would never forgive myself. But the thought of abandoning her in a nursing home so far away from me was abhorrent. So, after much soul-searching and praying to have her with me for at least two years, we brought her to live with us in Friendswood, Texas.

For the past sixteen years, since her stroke, I had written my mother every day. Lately my father had warned me she wasn't reading the letters and he feared she was "losing it." I sloughed off these observations, since to me she seemed fine. But I soon learned that she had rapidly advancing Alzheimer's.

We had great days and horrible days, weathering many problems. As Mother's illness progressed, her ups and downs became more extreme. She would be hyper for three days — always happy but unaware — then she'd go into what we called a "coma" for three days where we couldn't rouse her. Hospitalized many times, she always miraculously rallied and returned home to us.

Eventually, Mother lapsed into a coma and then developed pneumonia. The doctors and home healthcare nurses said death was imminent and that I should allow her to die at home. But after a sleepless night of listening to her death rales in the next room, I called the ambulance. She was taken to the hospital, where they said to prepare myself for her impending demise. How many times had I heard that?

Four days later, her doctor suggested we put her in a nursing home for her final days, again stressing the urgency of the situation. I reluctantly agreed; she had now been in a coma for a month. I visited her daily in her bright room and rang bells, shook clackers, even tap danced, doing my best to wake her, but to no avail.

She had been in the nursing home for over a month when I skipped my daily daytime visit. Since Art and I were taking dance lessons near the nursing home, we went to see her that evening after our lesson. When I walked into her room, she was sitting up, laughing and talking to a nurse. I couldn't believe my eyes.

She looked at me happily and said in a clear and distinct voice — one I had not heard for over seventeen years — "What are you doing here?" I couldn't believe my ears.

"We've been to our dance lesson," I stammered.

"Well, then, let's see what you learned."

We were in shock, but Art dutifully cleared the room of chairs and rolling tables, and we danced for my mother. I hummed the glorious foxtrot, waltz and swing ballroom music of her youth, while she kept time on the bed rail with her good left hand and giggled. I couldn't believe it.

After our impromptu recital, I asked her, "Do you know who I am?" She had not recognized me for many months.

Eyebrows arched, sighing, she slowly nodded her head. "Why, of course."

"Well, then, who am I?"

She couldn't understand why I was asking

such a silly question. "My daughter, Marilyn," she answered, a "shame-on-you" look on her face.

"Good! Who's this?" I pointed at Art. She had been unable to remember his name for a year, not to mention completely forgetting our last name.

Tired of such easy questions, she answered wearily, "Art Zapata."

We stood staring at her. Art recovered first and, giving her a kiss, said he was proud of her. She glowed. An incredible visit followed, reliving precious memories and family jokes — an unexpected gift.

As we prepared to leave, I said, "It's been great, Mother. I'll be back tomorrow."

She held up her finger and shook it, "Don't bother, honey. I'm going home."

"Sure," I said. "Now that you're better, you're coming back home with us."

"No," she persisted. "I'm going to my home. Joe is coming to pick me up tonight." She seemed really excited about this prospect, so I played along, not to spoil the mood.

"Well," I said, "tell him 'Hi' for me."

That night, the shrill ringing of the phone jarred me awake but I hesitated, fearing the news. Art stirred beside me, prodding me to answer. It was the nursing home calling to inform us that my mother, Dolly Bellinghausen, died during the night of natural causes, at the age of ninety.

I hung up the phone; there was a pause. Then in the darkness, Art softly asked, "Do you know what day it is?" I didn't. He said, "Think hard."

The realization struck me like lightning. I looked at the clock. It was March 23, 1994, 4:31 a.m. I took a deep breath and gathered my thoughts. It was two years to the day, to the hour, to the minute, that we had received the call that my father had died. My prayer had been answered, granting me exactly two extra years with my mother.

I can picture it now. Into my mother's room strides my tall father puffing white clouds of condensation. I see his breath evaporate into the warm room. Like many a scene from my youth, he wears a snowflake-sprinkled hat and tartan muffler wrapped securely around his neck. His left hand is gloved with a well-worn leather mitt and holds the glove's stiff mate. He blows into his clenched right fist, warming his exposed hand. I hear his car warming up outside. Then, pointing to his watch, he says for the last time, "Come on, Dolly. It's time. Let's go. We don't want to be late!"

~Marilyn Zapata

The Post-it Note

My bond with Papa grew stronger after he and Mom moved in with us after her fall. Two families living together wasn't easy, but soon I appreciated the blessings associated with day-in, day-out togetherness. Maybe that's why his death hit me so hard.

It seemed like no time since the strong, quiet man with the big smile was diagnosed with asbestosis, had lung surgery, and then moved into the nursing home for twenty-four-hour rehab care. One day, he said to me, "I'm never going home, am I?"

"I hope so, Papa," I answered, but we both knew it was unlikely.

He never asked again, and our lives revolved around Mom spending her days with him. I'd pop in for the night shift. Many times,

I brought work with me. He'd snooze, and I'd meet marketing deadlines — all within his curtained section of the room.

One night, Papa said, "You shouldn't work so much." He pointed a bony finger at my pile of notebooks, Post-it notes, proposals, and works-in-progress. Everything I needed to complete my projects except my laptop, which remained in the car. I didn't want to be so obvious about working. But Papa knew each time my BlackBerry dinged a message.

"You've got Post-it notes stuck on everything," he said, grinning.

"My memory isn't what it used to be," I said to him with a smile. "They remind me what's important to do."

"Just remember there's a difference between important to do and what's important." He patted my hand and lingered a beat.

To lighten the mood, he spent the rest of our visit teasing me about my Type A personality traits, something he swore I got from my mama. At the end of the night, he said, "Take it one day at a time, and you'll be fine. I do, and it works for me … with help from our Lord." His bright blue eyes twinkled. "Maybe you should make a note about that."

"Maybe I should," I said and laughed. "I'll remember … Don't be so serious. Be happy. Be happy. Be happy." I giggled, drew a smiley face, and printed his name, Delmar Ayers, above it. I slapped it against the pocket of his pajamas. He chuckled, and then he reminisced about dates with Mom. I updated him about my daughter Meredith's college life. He shared WWII stories. He said he'd like to go fishing again.

When I got to the car, I wrote on a sticky note: fishing trip for Papa — doable?

But the Coastal Georgia January weather turned cold and windy. The fishing trip had to wait.

On a cloudless, blue-sky Friday, Papa's lung specialist called Mom and me into his office. We studied a large mass on the screen. "There's nothing we can do," he said. "I've operated on folks older than eighty-six, but Mr. Ayers isn't a good candidate." We agreed not to tell him. "It will only depress him," the doctor said.

Instead, we spent the afternoon planning the fishing trip. We ate a burger. We talked about everything except lung cancer.

Over the weekend, EMS brought Papa to the hospital with sirens blaring, and he didn't regain consciousness. He struggled to breathe. "We'll try to keep him comfortable" resounded through the room. Mom and I huddled together, shell-shocked, after learning the cancer had spread into his stomach. The doctor contacted hospice. We stayed with Papa day and night.

The hospice nurse said, "His pulse reacts to your voice. He can hear you, so talk to him and share what's in your heart."

We poured out our love and memories while Papa's chest thrust up, then plummeted with raspy, ragged breathing. I turned to the nurse and said, "He was the best dad." And

Papa breathed his last breath.

He died on Wednesday, and I had no idea how hard the finality of it would hit me. Why hadn't I made his fishing trip happen? Spent more time with him? Why hadn't I…? The list went on and on.

Family and friends rallied around us. "He's in a better place," someone said. "He's not suffering now." Another friend shared a story about how a bird started showing up after her father's death. "Daddy was a florist," she said. "We decorated for Christmas together, and I missed him more than ever during the holidays. Still do," she admitted. "But I started noticing a bird hanging around. Once, I took the truck to get a large potted tree, and the bird landed on the back of the truck. It wouldn't get off. I knew Dad was with me."

I prayed for my own message from heaven.

A week later, we'd planned to spend Meredith's twenty-first birthday at her North Carolina college, a six-hour drive for us. I said to Mom, "I don't have enough energy to drive, but we have to go... I want to."

So I stood by the car and studied my list. I'd picked up Papa's belongings from the nursing home at daybreak, sobbing so much I had to pull off the road. I marked it off, but my heart sank. How could Mom and I get it together enough to celebrate this major milestone? I sighed and focused on the list: birthday cake, candles, Meredith's presents, camera, and other items waiting to be placed in the just-vacuumed car trunk.

I heaved our suitcases and pushed them to the back of the trunk, leaving ample room in the front part for our toiletry cases and birthday paraphernalia.

"Check the mailbox," Mom called from the door. "I forgot yesterday."

I walked down the driveway, shivering against February's biting wind. A bird flew in front of me, landed on our mailbox, and didn't move when I approached. I walked around the gray-brown bird, staring, but he ignored my movements. All of a sudden, he sang. Was it

Papa? I grabbed my camera from the car and took picture after picture from every angle before I went to get the rest of our stuff.

When I returned to the car, the bird landed in a nearby tree. I lifted the trunk lid, and gasped, staring at the empty space I had left in the trunk. The yellow sticky note with Delmar Ayers and a smiley face beamed like a ray of sun from heaven. My heart thudded. Memories of a younger, smiling Papa flowed through me, bringing a sense of peace. I looked around and the bird flew away as I slammed the car trunk shut.

"One day at a time," I promised. "Mom and I will be fine. I'll make a note of it."

~Debra Ayers Brown

The Littlest Things

One Friday at the end of a particularly hard and stressful week, an employee named JoAnn came to me and wanted to talk. She said she just felt "blah" for the past several weeks.

"It is very difficult to care about anything anymore, not just the little things but even the big things," she said. Little did she know that I was somewhere beyond that same point.

Her statement, though, took me back three months, when our family had lost a close friend. Zella was related to both sides of my family in various, complicated ways, and was like a sparkling extra grandmother to my children. She had a wonderful, hearty laugh combined with a glimmer in her eyes as she smiled. Zella had a hard life, but was positive and wise in her approach to life.

"Sometimes the littlest things make all the difference," she occasionally told me. She saw signs of God in those little, everyday things, whether it be her garden, her rock collection, or the chickens that she raised.

But I found myself beside Zella's bed in an intensive care unit, holding her hand while her children took a break from their vigil. A surgery the day before had revealed a huge mass involving most of her abdominal organs. There was nothing to be done. As Zella and her family hovered in that no man's land between hope and reality, I wanted to impart to her that God cared for her. I asked if she would like a prayer. Zella nodded yes. I had intended to recite the twenty-third Psalm, but realized I could not — I was totally blank! I was able to stumble through one prayer: The Lord's Prayer.

In the past Zella and I had talked about my infamous inability to memorize, and I had told her how I had tried often to memorize the twenty-third Psalm, but had never been able. As I sat beside her, a faint sparkle returned to her eyes along with a weak smile. She squeezed my hand. I knew that in normal times Zella and I would be laughing, in a kind way, about my awkwardness at that moment and how I had botched the prayer. But these were not normal times, and she slipped into unconsciousness the next day and died several days later.

The twenty-third Psalm is familiar to those of us from the Judeo-Christian tradition. It begins with "The Lord is my shepherd ..." and is perhaps the most recited Biblical verse. I would wager everyone from that background could think of someone they love or loved very much to whom this verse was important. It is common at funerals, and in times of danger and stress.

I made a renewed pledge to memorize it and tried for weeks. I printed it out in a large font and tried to memorize it while driving each day to work. It was a small miracle that I didn't cause a serious accident. But it just would not stick in my memory.

I became increasingly annoyed and, with

disgust, set the prayer aside. Many extra hours at work, the everyday stress of raising children, helping aged relatives and an overly busy life lead to a slow, darkening spiral that I hardly noticed. Over the weeks I became unfocused, and increasing felt ineffectual in many aspects of my life.

So there I was on that Friday night at the end of a long workday, with a woman who needed reassurance, who needed support, who needed motivation. And I was not sure I had any of those things to give. Without great enthusiasm I started one of my standard pep talks.

"You know, JoAnn, it isn't the job that you do that is important, it is how you do your job…" It sounded incredibly trite as I said it.

I encouraged her to care, because with caring comes hope. And where there is hope, there is always a future, a better day. I threw in an impromptu example of how easy it was not to care.

I said, "If you saw a piece of trash in the hallway, it would be easy not to pick it up. You could say, 'it is not my job.' But how much better it is to care. How much more positive it would be to pick up the trash. By thinking and acting positively, you helped a co-worker in a small way, and you helped yourself. Sometimes it is the little things that make all the difference in life."

I was not sure it was a convincing speech for JoAnn and I was certain it didn't convince me. I felt even more tired, more spent. It was as if what little bit of hope, if any, I had given to JoAnn was drained from me, leaving me with none.

I gathered my coat, and walked head bowed and disheartened down the hall. As I turned down a hallway, I passed a small rectangular piece of paper on the floor.

I just kept walking.

I walked about six paces beyond the paper, musing about the irony of the example I had just given my co-worker. But I didn't really want to stop, let alone turn, retrace my steps, and pick up the trash. But I did stop, and stood still for a moment — debating. Sighing, I turned back to the paper.

It was plain white and about one and a half inches wide and four inches long. As I picked it up, I realized it was a bookmark. When I turned it over, in small print, this is what was on the other side:

The Lord is my shepherd: I shall not want.

He maketh me to lie down in green pastures:

He leadeth me beside the still waters.

He restoreth my soul:

He leadeth me in the paths of righteousness for his name's sake.

Yea, though I walk through the valley of the shadow of death,

I will fear no evil for thou art with me:

Thy rod and thy staff they comfort me.

Thou preparest a table before me in the presence of mine enemies:

Thou anointest my head with oil; my cup runneth over.

Surely goodness and mercy shall follow me all the days of my life:

And I will dwell in the house of the Lord forever.

That was a pivotal point for me. It broke my mood and for some odd reason, or perhaps some not so odd reason, I was able to memorize the twenty-third Psalm easily after that day. And that day, and every day I hear that prayer now, I also sense Zella's twinkling eyes and laughter.

Every day we are presented with opportunities, some large, some small, to move forward in life's journey. I can tell you many times when opportunity knocks at our door, we don't open it to see what is there. Many times when a gift is placed at our feet, we don't stop and stoop to pick it up. But I've learned we should, even the littlest of gifts.

~Dan Reust

Otherworldly Answers

How does God, or Spirit or Jehovah or Krishna, depending on our personal belief system, decide when it's time for us to learn another lesson about life? Is it when we become too complacent, too sure we have all the answers? Answers not just to our own life's questions, but also to those of our family and friends?

The sign outside the large, old Victorian house read "Psychic Science Spiritualist Church." I had promised myself for years that someday I'd check it out. But if it hadn't been January, with little to look forward to until spring, if my friend Susanne hadn't been looking for diversion to take her mind off a failed romance, if I hadn't run into a couple at a Christmas party who had declared it fascinating, I probably wouldn't have been sitting in a wooden pew in the old house one Thursday evening.

The room was suggestive of the good parlor in grandmother's house, smelling not unpleasantly of furniture polish and old plaster dust. It had beamed ceilings and was lined with windows. Potted plants and ceramic figures of angels decorated the wide windowsills. A raised stage with a small piano, a lectern and several chairs took up one corner, and the empty fireplace under an ornate mantle attested to the house's domestic past. The entire house had that surface shabbiness generally indicative of limited resources, and there was definitely nothing otherworldly about it.

A dozen or so ordinary-looking people were scattered throughout the rows of pews. I glanced at one of the pamphlets I'd grabbed on the way in. "Serving the Indianapolis Community since 1923." I tried to dredge up any information I could remember about the Spiritualist movement, but pictured only séances and floating tables.

One of the pamphlets listed the nine principles of Spiritualism that had been established by the National Spiritualist Association of Churches. That information lent an aura of legitimacy to the group that I hadn't expected. The second surprise was that most of the principles sounded so normal, so similar to many slightly liberal Christian denominations. Excepting the one about spirits continuing to communicate with the living.

We sang several songs from the Spiritualist Hymnal, which looked a lot like the Methodist Hymnal of my youth. The realization that the Spiritualists had their own hymnal reminded me that this little group was part of a larger entity, a network that had been in existence for over a hundred years. Maybe not exactly flourishing, but still around.

The speaker, Bob Bianchi, led another Spiritualist church in Illinois. His talk, a pep talk for living our convictions, could have been given to many traditional church groups. Entertaining but hardly unique.

When he finished, his wife Sharon took the stage and started giving short readings to random members of the congregation, mentioning the name of a departed spirit as the source for each one. The messages sounded like the generic daily horoscopes in our local newspaper, and I could only concentrate for so long before my thoughts drifted to my own family problems.

My father, in his late eighties, needed round-the-clock care, and had recently entered a nursing home in his small Indiana town. He was not adjusting well, refusing all food and insisting that he was ready to die. But I couldn't just let him starve himself to death when he might live another few years with professional caretaking. He had a living will and a DNR order, but I knew that, as his healthcare proxy, I could override these documents. At a meeting with the doctor and nursing home administrator scheduled for the following day, I planned to ask for whatever it took to keep my father alive. Surely in time he would adjust to nursing home living.

As I was mulling over this problem, an image of an old photograph flashed through my mind — a photo of my maternal grandfather, William Franger, holding my three-year-old self in one arm and stroking the muzzle of a horse with the other. A rascal when he was younger, according to local legend, he'd been a bootlegger of regional renown back in the Prohibition era. Family history still includes tales about the prominent customers who drove down from Chicago to buy his "hooch." By the time I was born, though, he had become a prominent businessman whose opinion was respected in the community. He died when I was four years old and my memory of him is fuzzy, relying on old photos and stories more than actual recollection. But I've been told he called me his sweetheart child. Indeed, I'm sure I can remember sitting beside him on the porch swing while he sang "Let

Me Call You Sweetheart" just for me.

Now, in the hushed atmosphere of this religious organization, I realized I'd only ever heard him referred to as "Dad" or "Grandpa," never by his given name. Had he been called William, I wondered, or was he called Bill? I felt a wave of sadness, not only for my father's situation, but also for all the time with my grandfather I had missed and the wisdom he could have shared.

My thoughts were interrupted at this point when Bob, the speaker, took over the readings. He was giving a message to a man behind me when he stopped.

"I'm sorry, I'll get right back to you. First, I have someone here who needs to talk to... you." He looked directly at me. "His name is Bill, and he says to tell you they call him Bill, not William." He paused, seemed to listen, then repeated, "Bill, not William. And he says to tell you, about that problem, the right decision has already been made."

I was stunned. It was unfathomable that

Bob, or as he would have insisted, a spirit named Bill, was aware of my silent question and had given me a direct answer. My belief system was rocked. And I knew, in that moment, that I had no right to decide life or death for my father. As painful as it was, I had to let his decision stand.

My father died two weeks later from a case of pneumonia that his body was too weak to fight off. He seemed at peace at the end.

Spiritualism did not alter my belief system. I can't say I truly believe that an individual's existence and personal identity continues after death or that communication with the so-called dead is a fact. I do, however, now admit its possibility.

~Sheila Sowder

The Last Gift

The elementary school library was crawl-
ing with little ones, grabbing books and
crowding around the table where we worked.
We were the adult volunteers, moms mostly,
helping at the book fair. I sat next to a pretty
mom with blond hair, a foreign accent, and an
infectious smile. Her name was Lone, she said,
from Denmark. I had to ask her several times
how to say her name because here in Georgia,
we don't come across too many Danish folks.
A year later, Lone and her family moved a few
houses down from me, and despite the difference in cultures, we became fast friends. It was
hard not to be friends with Lone; she was
funny, and smart, and she'd do just about anything for you.

She was the person I could call, day or

night, when I was in a bind. It didn't matter what I needed: butter or milk for a recipe, tin foil for a school project, hair-braiding for my daughter, or sewing up a Halloween costume. Lone was one talented and generous friend, always happy to help. But it was her plant assistance that I especially relied upon.

You would think, coming from Denmark, that Lone's knowledge of plants would be limited to cold-weather varieties. But she knew everything about plants, what would thrive, what would wither, how and when to transplant, even Latin names! It was awesome to behold, to see Lone's yard and all her overflowing pots. She single-handedly turned my black thumb into a green thumb. We often went on plant-shopping expeditions, looking for the best deals. "Put that back and get this," she'd say. And I would. She had a knack for finding jewels among the dirt.

It was plants that brought her to my house one early October afternoon. I had a bed full of salvia and called to see if she'd like some of the plants I'd thinned out. She was in a hurry, but dashed down, and as usual, we started talking. We laughed, we talked some more, just an ordinary afternoon.

But a few weeks later, when her husband showed up at our door, asking to speak with my husband and me, I knew that the situation was anything but ordinary. That's when I found out that Lone was desperately ill.

She hadn't been feeling very well, said her husband. Though she'd never mentioned a word to me, not that afternoon or ever. Finally, she'd been in so much pain that she'd gone to the hospital. She was diagnosed with pancreatic cancer and there was little the doctors could do. She would try whatever treatment was available, he said, but the situation looked grim. For the present, she didn't want to see anyone. She had asked her husband to let me know.

"Can I call?" I asked, in tears.

"Not now," he said. She'd call when she felt better. November came and went. I brought

food and cards, but Lone never felt well
enough to see me. She never called. And a
week before Christmas, on a bitterly cold
night, she died. One of her daughters called
and asked me to come down. There, at last, I
saw my friend of fifteen years. But of course,
she'd already gone.

It was a shock to lose Lone. And worse, I
never had a chance to say goodbye, to tell her
what a wonderful friend she'd been to me, to
thank her for her kindness and generosity, to
let her know how honored I'd been to call her
friend. I knew she'd read my cards, where I'd
tried to express those feelings, but I'm not very
good at that sort of thing. I ached with the
pang of words gone unsaid.

The family took her body back to Denmark
for burial; a small memorial service was held
for her here. The weeks passed, and like the
snow we had here in Georgia, my acute grief
began to melt, too.

And then the weather warmed and the
spring rains fell and I looked out to the yard

where green grass poked through the dead leaves and suddenly I missed Lone so! We used to check with each other on the progress of our plants in the spring, as if our hostas were engaged in some kind of growth competition. But this year, I could barely bring myself to go outside. Spring had returned in all its glory but it seemed bleak without Lone by my side.

Then one morning, I awoke close to tears. I immediately went downstairs to tell my husband about a dream. Though even then, I knew what I'd experienced had been more than a dream.

I'd seen Lone at a crowded train station, her figure shadowy and distant. I couldn't believe my good fortune! There she was, if I could just catch up to her. But as I looked around, I began to realize that perhaps I was the only one who could see my friend. People rushed about around her, oblivious to her, all running to make their train. I knew she'd died, yes, I remembered that as I watched her thread through men and women. But still, here was my opportunity and I was determined to speak to her. I saw her duck into a shop and browse through overcoats, and it occurred to me that Lone was being her practical self. It's so very cold in Denmark! I crossed over to the other side of the tracks and walked into the shop.

"Lone!" I cried.

She turned and looked at me, with that infectious smile I knew so well. I ran to her and wrapped my arms around her.

"I love you so much!" I blurted, and I started to cry.

Now, I'm not a terribly demonstrative person. Neither was Lone. The truth is, we'd never say that to each other, in words. But in this dream, no, in this visit, I could say what was in my heart: "I love you so much!"

She hugged me, too, then looked at me with such understanding and a little half-smile.

"I know," she said.

That's when I awoke, and rushed to find my husband. I broke down and sobbed as I recounted what I'd shared with Lone. My husband didn't understand, didn't know quite what to do. He thought I was upset, but in truth, I was overwhelmed with joy and gratitude. Because that visit was just so typical of my friend.

I'm absolutely certain that Lone knew how desperately I needed to speak those words. And she came back to me, for only a brief moment, so that I could move on. You see, she couldn't go without helping me, one last time.

~Cathy C. Hall

Meet Our Contributors

Margo Berk-Levine went from actress/ model to founder/owner of a successful New York staffing company to writer. This is her second appearance in a *Chicken Soup for the Soul* book. Her stories have been in the *Scribblers' Journal*, as well as magazines. Works in progress include a series of short stories and a memoir. E-mail her at mberklevin@aol.com.

Jeanne Blandford has found her dream job as an editor at Chicken Soup for the Soul. When she is not reading inspirational submissions, she and her husband, Jack, are visiting their two children; working on documentaries; writing and producing children's books or volunteering for OPIN, a local animal rescue.

Debra Ayers Brown, a marketing profes-sional, received her B.A. degree with honors from the University of Georgia and her MBA degree from The Citadel. Visit her at DebraAy-ersBrown.com and link to her blogs: Slice of Coastal Life, Southern Deb, and My Yellow Bluff. E-mail her at dabmlb@comcost.net.

Terri Elders, LCSW, lives near Colville, WA, with two dogs and three cats. Her stories have appeared in multiple editions of *Chicken Soup for the Soul*. She's a public member of the Washington State Medical Quality Assurance Commission. Contact her via e-mail at telders@hotmail.com and read her blog atou-choftarragon.blogspot.com.

Cathy C. Hall is a writer from the sunny South. Her essays, stories, poetry, and articles have been published in markets for both kids and adults. Come visit her online to find out what she's working on now! You'll find her blog at www.cathychall.blogspot.com.

Christy Johnson, dynamic speaker and author of *Rehab for Love Junkies*, is passionate about sharing the hope of Christ. After a disastrous first marriage ended in adultery and the tragic death of her son, Christy has a passion to empower others to become soul-healthy. Visit her at www.christyjohnson.org.

Dan Reust lives and writes in the Denver, CO area. Contact him via e-mail at danreust@msn.com.

A former advertising executive, **Sheila Sowder** currently writes from a motorhome while traveling the country with her husband. Her stories have appeared in several editions of *Chicken Soup for the Soul*, and she is the author of *O'Toole's Irregulars (A Neighborhood Bar Mystery)*. Contact her via e-mail at sksowder@aol.com.

Donna Teti loves her life in Pennsylvania as a wife, mother, aunt, writer and speaker. She also loves being a teacher's assistant to adorable four-year-olds at Goshen Friends School. She has been previously published in *Guideposts*, *Christmas Miracles* and Chicken Soup for the Soul. Her website is donnateti.com.

Lisa Wojcik teaches literacy and art to low-income elementary grade children through a Florida public library system. Degreed from the University of New Mexico, Lisa is a science researcher, artist, and writer. Her short stories, poetry, children's literature, and research work can be seen at www.t4studios-bd.blogspot.com. E-mail her at lisawojcik@hotmail.com.

Marilyn Zapata works as a transcriber for court reporters. Her major client is her husband, Art, and after forty years of service, she has achieved tenure and cannot be fired. To view her other, more artistic pursuits, including a four-volume tome of their travels, visit marilynzapata.blogspot.com.

Meet Our Authors

Jack Canfield is the co-creator of the *Chicken Soup for the Soul* series, which *Time* magazine has called "the publishing phenomenon of the decade." Jack is also the co-author of many other bestselling books.

Jack is the CEO of the Canfield Training Group in Santa Barbara, California, and founder of the Foundation for Self-Esteem in Culver City, California. He has conducted intensive personal and professional development seminars on the principles of success for more than a million people in twenty-three countries, has spoken to hundreds of thousands of people at more than 1,000 corporations, universities, professional conferences and conventions, and has been seen by millions more on national television shows.

Jack has received many awards and honors,

including three honorary doctorates and a Guinness World Records Certificate for having seven books from the *Chicken Soup for the Soul* series appearing on the *New York Times* bestseller list on May 24, 1998.

You can reach Jack at
www.jackcanfield.com.

Mark Victor Hansen is the co-founder of Chicken Soup for the Soul, along with Jack Canfield. He is a sought-after keynote speaker, bestselling author, and marketing maven. Mark's powerful messages of possibility, opportunity, and action have created powerful change in thousands of organizations and millions of individuals worldwide.

Mark is a prolific writer with many bestselling books in addition to the *Chicken Soup for the Soul* series. Mark has had a profound influence in the field of human potential through his library of audios, videos, and articles in the areas of big thinking, sales achievement, wealth building, publishing success, and personal and professional development. He is also the founder of the MEGA Seminar Series.

Mark has received numerous awards that honor his entrepreneurial spirit, philanthropic heart, and business acumen. He is a lifetime member of the Horatio Alger Association of Distinguished Americans.

You can reach Mark at
www.markvictorhansen.com.

Amy Newmark was a writer, speaker, Wall Street analyst and business executive in the worlds of finance and telecommunications for more than thirty years. Today she is publisher, editor-in-chief and coauthor of the Chicken Soup for the Soul book series. By curating and editing inspirational true stories from ordinary people who have had extraordinary experiences, Amy has kept the twenty-one-year-old Chicken Soup for the Soul brand fresh and relevant, and still part of the social zeitgeist.

Amy graduated *magna cum laude* from Harvard University where she majored in Portuguese and minored in French. She wrote her thesis about popular, spoken-word poetry in Brazil, which involved traveling throughout Brazil and meeting with poets and writers to collect their stories. She is delighted to have come full circle in her writing career—from collecting poetry "from the people" in Brazil as a twenty-year-old to, three decades later, collecting stories and poems "from the people" for Chicken Soup for the Soul.

Amy has a national syndicated newspaper column and is a frequent radio and TV guest, passing along the real-life lessons and useful tips she has picked up from reading and editing thousands of Chicken Soup for the Soul stories.

She and her husband are the proud parents of four grown children and in her limited spare time, Amy enjoys visiting them, hiking, and reading books that she did not have to edit.

Sharing Happiness, Inspiration, and Wellness

Real people sharing real stories, every day, all over the world. In 2007, *USA Today* named *Chicken Soup for the Soul* one of the five most memorable books in the last quarter-century. With over 100 million books sold to date in the U.S. and Canada alone, more than 200 titles in print, and translations into more than forty languages, "chicken soup for the soul" is one of the world's best-known phrases.

Today, twenty-one years after we first began sharing happiness, inspiration and wellness through our books, we continue to delight our readers with new titles, but have also evolved beyond the bookstore, with wholesome and balanced pet food, delicious nutritious comfort food, and a major motion picture in development. Whatever you're doing, wherever you are, Chicken Soup for the Soul is "always there for you™." Thanks for reading!

Share with Us

We all have had Chicken Soup for the Soul moments in our lives. If you would like to share your story or poem with millions of people around the world, go to chickensoup.com and click on "Submit Your Story." You may be able to help another reader, and become a published author at the same time. Some of our past contributors have launched writing and speaking careers from the publication of their stories in our books!

We only accept story submissions via our website. They are no longer accepted via mail or fax.

To contact us regarding other matters, please send us an e-mail through webmaster@chickensoupforthesoul.com, or fax or write us at:

Chicken Soup for the Soul
P.O. Box 700
Cos Cob, CT 06807-0700
Fax: 203-861-7194

One more note from your friends at Chicken Soup for the Soul: Occasionally, we receive an unsolicited book manuscript from one of our readers, and we would like to respectfully inform you that we do not accept unsolicited manuscripts and we must discard the ones that appear.

A Taste of Chicken Soup for the Soul: Messages from Heaven
Miraculous Stories of Signs from Beyond, Amazing Connections,
and Love that Doesn't Die

Jack Canfield, Mark Victor Hansen & Amy Newmark

Published by Chicken Soup for the Soul Publishing, LLC
www.chickensoup.com

The publisher gratefully acknowledges the many publishers and
individuals who granted Chicken Soup for the Soul permission to
reprint the cited material.

Front cover photo courtesy of iStockphoto.com/Liliboas
(© Lisa Thornberg).

Library of Congress Control Number: 2011942715

A Taste of ISBN: 978-1-61159-864-3

Full Book ISBN: 978-1-935096-91-7

A Taste of
Chicken Soup for the Soul®

Messages from Heaven

*Miraculous Stories of Signs from
Beyond, Amazing Connections,
and Love that Doesn't Die*

Jack Canfield
Mark Victor Hansen
Amy Newmark

Chicken Soup for the Soul Publishing, LLC
Cos Cob, CT